Oxford Read and Discover

6

All About Space

Alex Raynham

Contents

OXFORD
UNIVERSITY PRESS

UNIVERSITY PRESS

Great Clarendon Street, Oxford OX2 6DP

Oxford University Press is a department of the University of Oxford. It furthers the University's objective of excellence in research, scholarship, and education by publishing worldwide in

Oxford New York

Auckland Cape Town Dar es Salaam Hong Kong Karachi Kuala Lumpur Madrid Melbourne Mexico City Nairobi New Delhi Shanghai Taipei Toronto

With offices in

Argentina Austria Brazil Chile Czech Republic France Greece Guatemala Hungary Italy Japan Poland Portugal Singapore South Korea Switzerland Thailand Turkey Ukraine Vietnam

OXFORD and OXFORD ENGLISH are registered trade marks of Oxford University Press in the UK and in certain other countries

© Oxford University Press 2010

The moral rights of the author have been asserted

Database right Oxford University Press (maker)

First published 2010

2022

20

No unauthorized photocopying

ISBN: 978 0 19 464560 7

An Audio Pack containing this book and an Audio download is also available, ISBN 978 0 19 402235 4

This book is also available as an e-Book, ISBN 978 0 19 464735 9

An accompanying Activity Book is also available, ISBN 978 0 19 464570 6

Printed in China

This book is printed on paper from certified and well-managed sources.

ACKNOWLEDGEMENTS

Illustrations by: Kelly Kennedy pp.9, 11, 21; Ian Moores Graphics pp.5, 12; Dusan Pavlic/Beehive Illustration pp.40, 44, 46; Alan Rowe pp.40, 44, 46.

The Publishers would also like to thank the following for their kind permission to reproduce photographs and other copyright material: Alamy pp.21 (World History Archive), 24 (TCD/ Prod DB © Warner Bros MARS ATTACKS), 30 (space shuttle/ RGB Ventures/Superstock, ISS/Newscom), 31 (Granger Historical Picture Archive); GalacticSuite.com p.32; Getty Images p.20 (Khaled Desouki/AFP); Mary Evans Picture Library p.22 (Galileo); NASA Images pp.4 (NASA/ESA/The Hubble Heritage/Team (STScI/AURA) J. Blakeslee (JHU) and R. Thompson (University of Arizona)), 5-6 (Lunar and Planetary Laboratory/NASA images/solar system), 6 (Mars Twin Peaks), 8, 10, 13, 14 (NASA/JPL/Space Science Institute), 15, 16 (NASA/JPL-Caltech/T. Pyle (SSC)), 23 (Eagle Nebula Hubble Space photo/T.A.Rector (University of Alaska Anchorage, NRAO/AUI/NSF and NOAO/AURA/NSF) and B.A.Wolpa (NOAO/AURA/NSF)), 25 (Mars Rover), 26 (NASA/ Goddard Space Flight Center Scientific Visualization Studio), 29 (David R. Scott), 33 (JSC/NASA Images), 34 (robonaut/ NASA Images), 35 (Denise Watt/NASA Images/asteroid mining), 38 (Lunar and Planetary Laboratory/NASA images); Oxford University Press p.3 (earth/Corbis, moon/Stockbyte, sun/Comstock/Getty, Saturn/Photodisc/Getty), 9, 11, 17, 23 (Hubble telescope), 27 (UFO), (star background used on pp.8, 9, 10, 13, 14, 15, 26/Photodisc/Getty); Science Photo Library p.3, (Hale Bopp over observatory/David Nunuk), 18 (David Parker), 19 (Richard Bizley), 22 (Milky Way/Allan Morton/Dennis Milon), 25 (bacteria/Dr Kari Lounatmaa), 26 (Titan/NASA/JPL/Space Science Institute), 27 (Gliese 581/ David A. Hardy), 28 (Sputnik).

Introduction

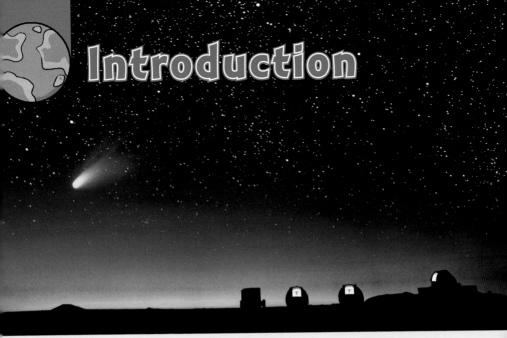

Space is everything that's around planet Earth, and it's bigger than we can imagine. When you look at the sky at night, you can see thousands of stars. Did you know that the Sun is a star, too? There are also billions of other stars in space, and billions of planets!

How many planets do you know?
What do you know about them?
What can you see below?

1 2 3 4

Discover!

Now read and discover more about space!

Stars are huge balls of hot gas. A star with planets around it is called a solar system. Our Sun has eight planets – this is our solar system.

Our Galaxy

Groups of stars are called galaxies. Each galaxy has billions of stars. Our solar system is in a galaxy called the Milky Way that has 200 billion stars. There are billions of other galaxies in the universe.

Galaxies in Space

Discover! The universe is everything that exists – all the stars in all the galaxies. It appeared in a single moment, called the Big Bang, about 14 billion years ago. Before then, there were no stars.

Our Amazing Sun

The Sun and all other stars are made of two gases called hydrogen and helium. The hydrogen changes into helium in a process called nuclear fusion. This process produces heat and light. Our Sun is about 150 million kilometers away from Earth, but it's hot enough to burn you at the beach! Plants on Earth use energy from the Sun to grow. Animals and people also get their energy from the Sun because they eat plants.

Earth and the Sun

A planet goes around, or orbits, a star. It takes our planet Earth one year to orbit the Sun. A planet also turns on its axis. It takes Earth 24 hours to do a complete turn on its axis. When a place on Earth is opposite the Sun, it's daytime in that place.

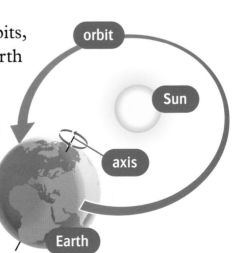

orbit

Sun

axis

Earth

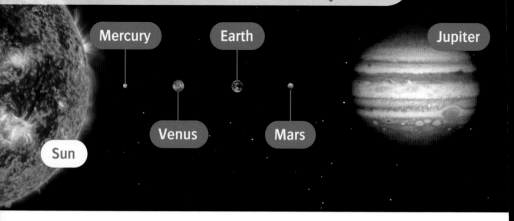

The Planets in Our Solar System

Mercury

Earth

Jupiter

Venus

Mars

Sun

All the planets in our solar system orbit the Sun. A year is the time that it takes a planet to orbit the Sun – it's 365 days for Earth. Mercury and Venus are near the Sun, so they have shorter years because they travel a shorter distance around the Sun. A year on Mercury is the same as 88 days on Earth. Planets that are further from the Sun have longer orbits. A year on Neptune is the same as 165 years on Earth.

Rocks and Soil on Mars

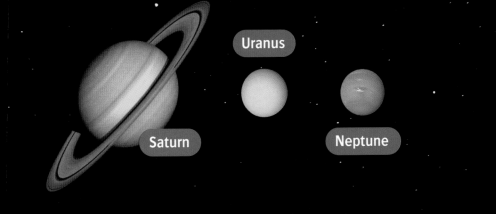

Each planet in our solar system is different, but Mercury, Venus, and Mars are rocky planets like Earth. If you landed on these planets, you would find rocks, and you could walk around on them.

Jupiter, Saturn, Uranus, and Neptune are called gas giants. They are much bigger than the rocky planets, and they are made mostly of gas.

Dwarf Planets

Astronomers have discovered five dwarf planets in our solar system. Dwarf planets are like very small planets and they orbit the Sun. The biggest dwarf planet is called Eris, and it's 2,500 kilometers across.

The most famous dwarf planet is Pluto. It was discovered in 1930, and for more than 70 years, it was called the ninth planet in the solar system. Now it's called a dwarf planet.

Go to pages 36–37 for activities.

2 The Inner Planets

The inner planets in our solar system are Mercury, Venus, Earth, and Mars. They are the nearest planets to the Sun and they are made of rocks and soil. Venus, Earth, and Mars have gas around them, called atmosphere.

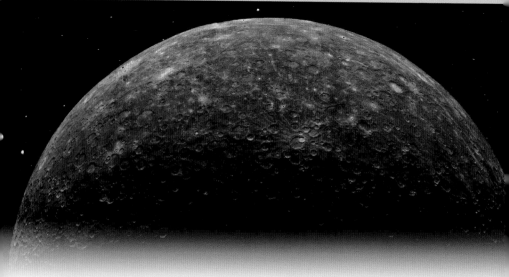

Mercury

Mercury is the smallest planet in the solar system and it doesn't have an atmosphere. A planet's atmosphere traps the Sun's heat, and keeps the temperature warm at night. Mercury is very hot in the daytime because it's the nearest planet to the Sun, but it's very cold at night. When the temperature on one half of Mercury is 427 degrees centigrade, the other half is minus 173 degrees!

Venus

Venus is the second planet from the Sun, and the nearest planet to Earth, but it would not be a nice place to visit! Pressure is the force or weight of something on your body. Venus has more gas in its atmosphere than Earth, and all that gas creates pressure. If astronauts visited Venus, the pressure would kill them.

In the atmosphere around Venus, a gas called carbon dioxide traps heat from the Sun. The temperature on Venus is 462 degrees centigrade – that's hotter than a pizza oven! The sky on Venus is yellow because there are clouds of sulphuric acid. This dangerous chemical can burn metal.

Discover!

Venus turns very slowly on its axis, but it orbits the Sun very quickly, so a day is longer than a year on Venus!

Earth

Earth is our home, and it's the third planet from the Sun. Billions of years ago, Earth was very hot. Later, the planet became cooler and oceans of water formed. Life began in these oceans about 3.5 billion years ago.

Earth is a great place for life because it isn't too hot or too cold for liquid water. Plants, animals, and people need liquid water to live, and they also need oxygen. Most of the gas in Earth's atmosphere is nitrogen, but 20.7% is oxygen.

A moon orbits a planet, and often looks like a small planet. Earth has one moon, but some planets have a lot. Our Moon takes 27 days to orbit Earth. Mars, Jupiter, Saturn, and Neptune all have moons, too.

Earth and Its Moon

Mars

Mars is the fourth planet from the Sun and it has two small moons. Mars is smaller than Earth and it's called the red planet because chemicals make the soil red.

Mars has some amazing places. Mons Olympus is a volcano, and it's 25 kilometers high! That's three times higher than Mount Everest, the highest mountain on Earth. The Valles Marineris is a huge canyon. It's ten times longer and three times deeper than the Grand Canyon, the biggest canyon on Earth!

The Valles Marineris Canyon, Mars

Discover!

Some scientists think that there were rivers on Mars in the past, but then the temperature became colder. Now all the water is ice.

Go to pages 38–39 for activities.

The four outer planets in our solar system are the farthest away from the Sun, and they are Jupiter, Saturn, Uranus, and Neptune. Do you know what they are made of?

Gas Giants

The outer planets are bigger than the inner planets, and they don't have a rocky surface. We call them gas giants because they are made of hydrogen, helium, and other gases around a rocky center. Inside these planets, pressure changes the gases into a liquid.

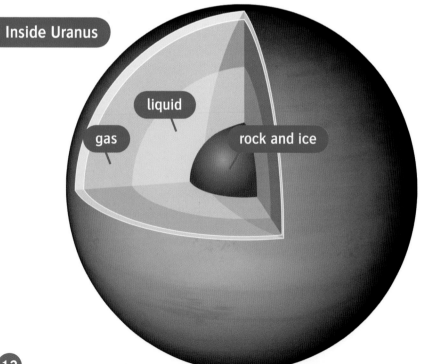

Inside Uranus

liquid

gas

rock and ice

Jupiter

Jupiter is the fifth planet from the Sun. It's the biggest planet in our solar system, and it's more than a thousand times bigger than Earth! Jupiter has about 60 moons, and some of them are bigger than planets.

Huge storms move clouds of gas around Jupiter, and they make beautiful colors in the atmosphere. Jupiter has a big red circle of storm clouds called the red spot. This is the biggest storm in our solar system. Storms on Earth can last for days, but this storm started 300 years ago and it hasn't finished yet!

Jupiter and Its Moons

Jupiter's red spot

Discover!

Jupiter and the other gas giants have a lot of moons. Scientists are discovering new moons all the time.

rings

Saturn is the second biggest planet in our solar system and the sixth planet from the Sun. There are thousands of rings around Saturn. The farthest ring is millions of kilometers from Saturn. The rings are made of billions of pieces of dust and ice. Some pieces of ice are very small, and some are bigger than houses. Saturn's rings are different colors because of chemicals in the ice.

Saturn has about 60 moons. The biggest moon is called Titan. Titan has atmosphere, clouds, and lakes, but the lakes are made of chemicals, not water.

Discover! Jupiter, Uranus, and Neptune also have rings, but they aren't as big or as beautiful as the rings around Saturn.

Uranus and Neptune

Uranus is the seventh planet in the solar system. It's 2.4 billion kilometers from the Sun! If you travel another 2 billion kilometers out into space, you will reach Neptune, the farthest planet from the Sun.

Uranus and Neptune are far from the Sun, so they are very cold. The temperature on Neptune is minus 214 degrees centigrade. Both planets are made mostly of gas, like Jupiter and Saturn, but different chemicals in their atmospheres make them green and blue. Uranus has 27 moons and Neptune has 13.

Neptune

→ Go to pages 40–41 for activities.

4 Rocks and Ice

There are two rings around the Sun, called the asteroid belt and the Kuiper belt. The asteroid belt is between Mars and Jupiter. It's made of rocks called asteroids. The Kuiper belt is further away than Neptune. It's made of pieces of ice.

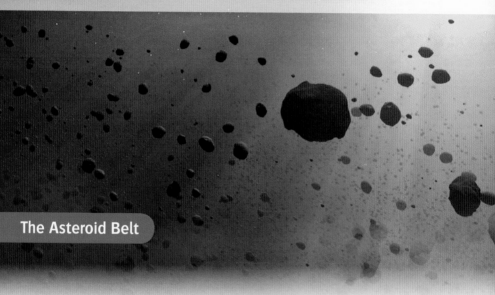

The Asteroid Belt

Asteroids

Some rocks in the asteroid belt are the size of houses, but others are many kilometers across. When planets come near them, or other asteroids hit them, these rocks can leave the asteroid belt. Sometimes, they travel toward the inner planets.

Comets

Comets are huge pieces of ice and dust, and some of them are 50 kilometers across. Comets come from the Kuiper belt, or from further away in space, but sometimes their orbits bring them nearer Earth and the Sun. When comets come nearer the Sun, they become hotter and they leave pieces of ice and dust behind them. This is called a comet's tail and it can be millions of kilometers long!

Halley's Comet in 1986

Discover!

Halley's Comet is a famous comet. It comes near Earth every 75 or 76 years. We will see it again in 2061.

Meteors and Meteorites

Meteors are pieces of rock, dust, or ice that enter a planet's atmosphere. They come from asteroids and comets.

Most meteors burn when they enter the atmosphere, but sometimes pieces hit a planet's surface and these pieces are called meteorites. More than 1,000 metric tons of ice, dust, and rocks from space land on Earth every year, but most of these pieces are very small.

Sometimes big meteorites hit Earth and make a huge hole called a crater. Big meteorites don't hit planets very often, but they are very dangerous. In 1994, 21 pieces of a comet hit Jupiter. Some of the explosions were bigger than our planet Earth!

A Meteorite Crater in Arizona, USA

In 1908, a meteorite exploded in the sky above the Tunguska River, in Siberia in Russia. No one lived there, but a forest of 80 million trees was burned.

About 65 million years ago, there were no people on Earth, and the animals were different, too. Dinosaurs lived here. Then one day a bright light appeared in the sky. It was a huge meteorite. Some of it burned in the atmosphere, but a piece hit Earth – it was about 20 kilometers long. The meteorite crater is in Chicxulub, in the Yucatan in Mexico, and it's 180 kilometers across!

When the meteorite hit Earth, there was a huge explosion. Scientists think that fires and acid destroyed most of the world's forests. Clouds of dust covered the sky, and light from the Sun didn't reach Earth's surface. It became very cold for many years. At about the same time, the dinosaurs and 70% of all the plants and other animals on Earth died.

The Chicxulub Meteorite

➔ Go to pages 42–43 for activities.

Astronomy is studying the planets and the stars, and people who study astronomy are called astronomers. Do you know what they have discovered?

Ancient Astronomers

Thousands of years ago, people in places like China, Iraq, and Greece used the Sun, the Moon, and the stars to calculate the time of year and the seasons. This is how they knew the dates of festivals and when to plant seeds. Many people, like the Ancient Egyptians or the Incas of South America, thought that the Sun was a god.
They built beautiful temples for the Sun.

Inside Abu Simbel Temple

Discover!

Sunlight falls on the statues in this Ancient Egyptian temple at sunrise on two days every year. These were important days in the Egyptian calendar.

Understanding the Solar System

Most ancient astronomers believed that Earth was at the center of our solar system. They thought that the Sun, the other stars, and all the planets orbited Earth.

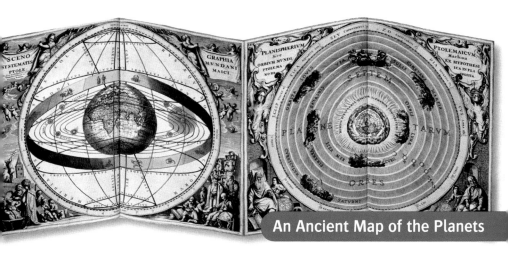

An Ancient Map of the Planets

In 1543, a Polish astronomer called Copernicus said that the Sun was at the center of our solar system, but people didn't believe him. Later, other astronomers like Galileo Galilei, from Pisa, now in Italy, believed him, but important people stopped them writing about their ideas. Almost 150 years later, a British astronomer called Isaac Newton proved that Earth orbits the Sun.

Isaac Newton discovered the force of gravity. Gravity makes things fall to the ground on Earth. It also makes the planets orbit the Sun.

Galileo and the First Telescopes

Telescopes help people to learn about our solar system. In 1609, Galileo used one of the first telescopes to look at the night sky. He saw mountains and craters on the Moon, and four moons around Jupiter. The first telescopes were very small. Later, people made bigger telescopes, and they discovered new planets and moons.

Our Galaxy and the Universe

When Galileo looked at a bright area in the night sky, he discovered that it was made of many stars. Later, people discovered that this is the center of our galaxy, the Milky Way. For a long time, astronomers thought that the Milky Way was the only galaxy in the universe. Then in 1930, an American astronomer called Edwin Hubble discovered another galaxy. Now we know that there are billions of galaxies in the universe.

The Center of the Milky Way

Astronomy Today

Today, astronomers use huge telescopes to study the stars. They can see the light from galaxies billions of kilometers from Earth. Astronomers use different telescopes to look for other types of energy from stars, called radio waves and X-rays. Astronomers also use spacecraft to explore our solar system. Spacecraft orbit or fly past other planets and take photos. Some spacecraft have visited other planets and moons, too.

Discover!

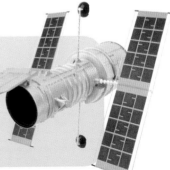

The Hubble Space Telescope has orbited Earth since 1990. It can take better photos than telescopes on Earth because it's outside Earth's atmosphere.

➜ Go to pages 44–45 for activities.

23

6 Life on Other Planets

In stories, aliens are living things from another world, but are they real? Is there life on other planets? Astronomers are looking for life in our solar system, and on planets around other stars.

Martians!

A hundred years ago, telescopes were smaller, and it was difficult to see Mars clearly. Astronomers thought that they saw lines on the surface of Mars, and some people thought that they were canals. At the time, people were building great canals on Earth, like the Panama Canal in Central America.

Some astronomers imagined aliens building these canals and living in cities on Mars. People wrote stories and made movies about aliens from Mars, called Martians, visiting Earth. Now we know that there aren't any Martians, but we still make movies about them!

Water and Bacteria

Life on Earth needs liquid water, carbon, and gases like oxygen and nitrogen. When scientists look for life on other planets, they look for places that have liquid water.

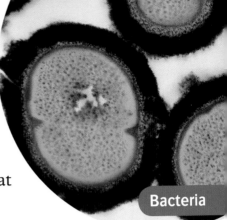

Bacteria

Bacteria are simple living things on Earth, and they can live in very hot and cold places, and even inside rocks. Scientists are looking for bacteria on Mars and in other places in our solar system.

Life on Mars

It's very cold on Mars, so all the water on the surface is ice. Many scientists think that there is liquid water in the soil or even in underground rivers. Maybe there is life on Mars, too. At the moment, robots from Earth are exploring Mars and looking for life.

A Robot on Mars

Europa

Europa is one of Jupiter's moons and it's covered in ice. The surface is very cold, but scientists think it's warmer inside. Maybe there are oceans under the ice. Maybe there are bacteria or other living things in the oceans, too. One day people will send robots to explore Europa and to look for life.

Titan

Saturn's largest moon, Titan, is the only moon in the solar system with atmosphere. It has rivers, lakes, rain, and clouds. These are made of chemicals called hydrocarbons, and scientists think that there is water under the surface of Titan, too. Living things are made of hydrocarbons and water. Maybe one day we will discover life on Titan.

Life in Other Solar Systems

What do we know about life in other solar systems? Astronomers have found hundreds of planets near other stars, but they are still looking for a planet like Earth. Some scientists think that there are lots of planets like Earth in our galaxy, and millions in the universe. Maybe there is life on some of them. On another planet billions of kilometers from here, maybe alien astronomers are looking at the stars!

Discover!

Sometimes, people see unusual objects in the sky, called UFOs. Some people think that they are alien spacecraft, but they are usually things like balloons or comets.

➜ Go to pages 46–47 for activities.

7 People in Space

More than 450 astronauts have seen Earth from space. They have done experiments, visited the Moon, and taught us a lot about our solar system. Would you like to travel in space?

The First Astronauts

In 1957, Russia sent the first rocket into space. It took a machine called a satellite. Then on 12th April 1961, another Russian rocket called *Vostok* carried a small spacecraft into space. Inside there was a man called Yuri Gagarin. He was the first person in space. His spacecraft orbited Earth for 108 minutes, and then returned to Earth. Later, Russia and America built bigger and better rockets, and more astronauts went into space.

Discover! Today, hundreds of satellites orbit Earth. We use them to study the weather, to take photos, and to do lots of other things.

Vostok in 1961

28

Astronauts on the Moon

In 1968, astronauts in the *Apollo 8* spacecraft orbited the Moon for the first time. Then, on July 21st 1969, the *Apollo 11* spacecraft landed on the Moon. Millions of people watched on television when two American astronauts called Neil Armstrong and Edwin 'Buzz' Aldrin stepped onto the Moon. It was an incredible moment – for the first time in history, people walked on another world.

Another ten American astronauts visited the Moon between 1969 and 1972. They did experiments and collected rocks and soil. They also drove a special car called a lunar rover, or moon buggy!

An Astronaut on the Moon in 1971

lunar rover

Space Shuttles

In 1981, a new type of spacecraft flew for the first time. It was called a space shuttle. Space shuttles can fly into space many times because they take off like a rocket and they land like a plane. They have taken very big things into space, like the Hubble Space Telescope.

Space Stations

A space station is a place in space where astronauts can live and do experiments. The first space stations were very small, but the International Space Station (ISS) is much bigger. It was built in space. The first astronauts visited it in 1998. Now, teams of astronauts from different countries live and work on the space station all the time.

The ISS

Living in Space

If you drop something on Earth, it falls to the ground because of gravity. In a spacecraft, astronauts don't feel gravity because their spacecraft is moving very fast. This is called zero gravity, and you can float!

In space, things float, so astronauts use a material called Velcro® to stick everything to the walls. Astronauts cook food in special containers, and they use a special shower because water floats, too. They also use special sleeping bags to stop them floating when they sleep!

Gravity makes you strong on Earth because you exercise your body every time you walk or lift something. Your body doesn't do this in space, so astronauts can become weak. They have to use exercise machines to keep strong.

Discover!

The ISS orbits Earth once every 90 minutes. It's difficult for astronauts to sleep because the Sun rises or sets every 45 minutes. Astronauts wear masks over their eyes.

→ Go to pages 48–49 for activities.

A hundred years ago, space travel was a dream. Now, people are living in space. What will happen in the next hundred or thousand years?

A Design for a Space Hotel

Space Tourism

A few tourists have already visited space, but their trips cost millions of dollars. Now, people have designed special space planes to take tourists into space. They are cheaper than rockets, but at the moment, space plane trips only last a few hours. In the future, maybe tourists will orbit Earth and stay in space hotels. Maybe they will enjoy amazing views of Earth from the hotel windows, and play games and sports in zero gravity, too!

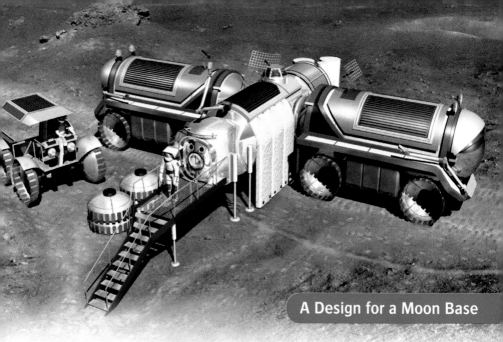

Living on the Moon

We are building new spacecraft to take people to the Moon. The first astronauts will visit the Moon in about 2020, and they will stay there for a week. Later, astronauts will build a Moon base. Scientists, engineers, and astronomers will live in the Moon base for months, so that they can do experiments. Living on the Moon won't be easy. Food and equipment will come from Earth, 386,000 kilometers away! There is no atmosphere on the Moon, so people will wear space suits to protect themselves when they go outside.

Discover!

The Sun produces a dangerous type of energy called radiation. Earth's atmosphere protects us, but scientists must find a way to protect people in the Moon base.

Exploring Mars

With today's spacecraft, it would take astronauts about two years to reach Mars and return to Earth. It would be very difficult to take enough food and water for such a long trip, and the Sun's radiation would be very dangerous, too.

In the future, scientists will probably invent faster spacecraft, and ways to protect the astronauts from radiation. The first astronauts will probably visit Mars in about 50 years from now.

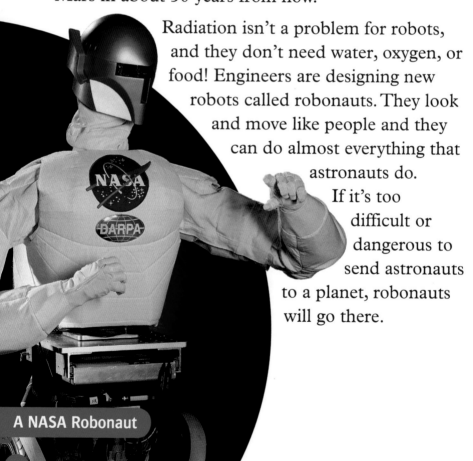

Radiation isn't a problem for robots, and they don't need water, oxygen, or food! Engineers are designing new robots called robonauts. They look and move like people and they can do almost everything that astronauts do. If it's too difficult or dangerous to send astronauts to a planet, robonauts will go there.

A NASA Robonaut

In a Thousand Years from Now

Maybe one day people will live on Mars or in huge space stations. There are lots of materials like metals, ice, and hydrocarbons in our solar system. We can use these materials to produce oxygen and water, and to grow food. We can also make fuel for rockets, and build new spacecraft. If we invent very fast spacecraft, maybe we will explore other solar systems one day, too.

A thousand years ago, people traveled by horse, and we didn't know that the world was round. In a thousand years from now, we will have new technologies and new ways to explore space. What do you think our life will be like? Where do you think we will live?

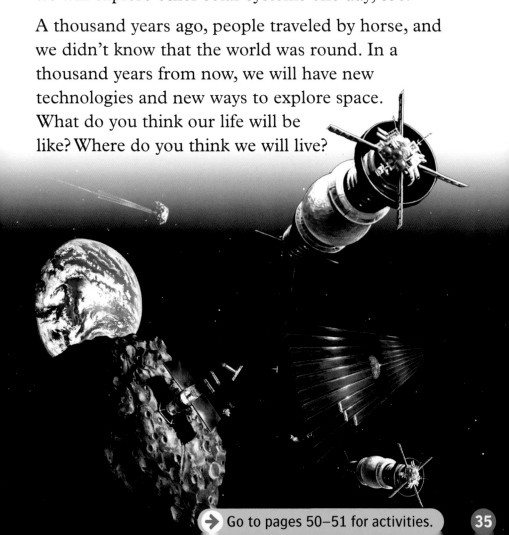

→ Go to pages 50–51 for activities.

1 Our Solar System

← Read pages 4–7.

1 Complete the sentences.

axis   solar   orbit   ~~galaxy~~

1 Our solar system is in a __galaxy__ called the Milky Way.

2 Stars with planets around them are called _____ systems.

3 All the planets in our solar system _____ the Sun.

4 A planet turns on its _____ .

2 Complete the puzzle. Write the secret word.

1 Planets, like Jupiter and Neptune, are called gas __ .
2 __ are huge balls of hot gas.
3 The Sun is made of hydrogen and __.
4 __ planets are like very small planets.
5 It takes Earth 24 hours to do a complete turn on its __ .
6 All plants on Earth get their __ from the Sun.

	1 →	g	i	a	n	t	s
2 →						
3 →						
4 →					
5 →			
6 →						

The secret word is:

3 Write the words in order, from smallest to biggest.

galaxy ~~dwarf planet~~ solar system planet universe star

1 dwarf planet   3 _____   5 _____

2 _____   4 _____   6 _____

4 Circle the correct words.

1 The Big Bang was about 14 **million** / **billion** years ago.

2 Dwarf planets orbit **the Sun** / **other planets**.

3 Mercury and Mars are made of **gas** / **rocks**.

4 Our galaxy has 200 **billion** / **million** stars.

5 Nuclear fusion produces light and **gas** / **heat**.

5 Answer the questions.

1 When is it daytime on Earth?

When a place on Earth is opposite the Sun.

2 What produces the heat on the Sun?

_____

3 Why is the Sun important for plants?

_____

4 Why do the planets that are nearer the Sun have
shorter years?

_____

5 What is the biggest dwarf planet, and how big is it?

_____

37

2 The Inner Planets

← Read pages 8–11.

1 Write the numbers. Then write the words.

Mars Venus ~~Mercury~~ Earth

1 ●	2 🌑	3 🌍	4 ●

Mercury [1]   Mars [ ]   Earth [ ]   Venus [ ]

1 This planet is red. <u>Mars</u>

2 This planet has a yellow sky. _____

3 This planet doesn't have an atmosphere. _____

4 This planet has oceans. _____

5 This planet has short years and long days. _____

6 This planet has some amazing places. _____

2 Write *true* or *false*.

1 Some planets have an atmosphere.   <u>true</u>

2 Mercury is very hot at night.   _____

3 The pressure on Venus is higher than on Earth.   _____

4 Earth is the nearest planet to the Sun.   _____

5 Plants and animals need liquid water.   _____

6 There is liquid water on Mars today.   _____

3 **Write the words.**

> carbon dioxide   temperature   atmosphere
> pressure   canyon   sulphuric acid

1 how hot something is   _____

2 the gas around a planet   _____

3 it's very deep   _____

4 a gas that traps heat from the Sun   _____

5 the force or weight of something on your body   _____

6 a dangerous chemical that can burn metal   _____

4 **Answer the questions.**

1 What are the inner planets made of?

_____

2 What are the clouds made of on Venus?

_____

3 Why is Earth a great place for life?

_____

4 How long does it take our Moon to orbit Earth?

_____

5 Why is the soil red on Mars?

_____

6 What do scientists think there was on Mars in the past?

_____

3 The Outer Planets

← Read pages 12–15.

1 Write the planets in the correct order, from nearest to farthest from the Sun.

Earth   Neptune   ~~Mercury~~   Saturn
Jupiter   Venus   Uranus   Mars

1   2   3   4   5   6   7   8

1 __Mercury__   4 _____   7 _____

2 _____   5 _____   8 _____

3 _____   6 _____

2 Write the words.

cloud   lake   ice   ring   rock   storm

1 _____

4 _____

2 _____

5 _____

3 _____

6 _____

3 Circle the correct words

1 Inside gas giants, pressure changes the gases into a liquid / cloud.

2 Jupiter's red spot is a huge **atmosphere** / **storm**.

3 The lakes on Titan are made of **chemicals** / **water**.

4 All of the gas giants have moons and **rocks** / **rings**.

5 Saturn is the **second** / **sixth** biggest planet.

4 Match.

1 The outer planets are called	made of ice.
2 Titan is one of	27 moons.
3 Jupiter is the biggest	farthest planet from the Sun.
4 Saturn's rings are	the gas giants.
5 Neptune is the	planet in the solar system.
6 Uranus has	Saturn's moons.

5 Answer the questions.

1 What is the difference between gas giants and rocky planets?

_____

2 Why are there different colors in Saturn's rings?

_____

3 Why is Neptune very cold?

_____

4 Rocks and Ice

← Read pages 16–19.

1 Write the words.

> meteor   comet   meteorite   asteroid

1 This is made of ice and dust.   _____

2 This is a big rock.   _____

3 This is a piece of rock, dust, or ice that enters the atmosphere.   _____

4 This is a piece of ice or rock that hits a planet.   _____

2 Complete the sentences.

> ice   crater   dinosaurs   tail   rings   rocks   burn

1 There are two _____ around the Sun.

2 The asteroid belt is made of _____ .

3 The Kuiper belt is made of pieces of _____ .

4 When a comet comes near the Sun, it has a _____ .

5 Most meteors _____ when they enter the atmosphere.

6 A big meteorite can make a _____ on Earth.

7 The _____ were big animals that lived a long time ago.

3 **Write _T_ for the Tunguska meteorite or _C_ for the Chicxulub meteorite.**

This meteorite …

1 hit Earth millions of years ago.   _C_

2 destroyed a forest.   ____

3 was about 20 kilometers long.   ____

4 killed a lot of animals.   ____

5 exploded in the sky.   ____

6 changed the weather for a long time.   ____

7 hit Russia about 100 years ago.   ____

4 **Correct the sentences.**

1 The asteroid belt is between Earth and the Sun.

   The asteroid belt is between Mars and Jupiter.

2 A lot of comets come from the asteroid belt.

   _____

3 Comets become colder when they are near the Sun.

   _____

4 We can see Halley's Comet in the sky all the time.

   _____

5 Some meteorites hit the Moon in 1994.

   _____

6 About 65 million years ago, there were no animals on Earth.

   _____

5 Astronomy

← Read pages 20–23.

1 Write the words.

telescope   temple   seeds   astronomer   spacecraft   calendar

 1 _____

 4 _____

 2 _____

 5 _____

 3 _____

 6 _____

2 Find and write the words.

f	e	s	t	i	v	a	l	e
o	x	i	s	g	n	i	o	t
r	f	j	k	a	p	c	x	e
c	a	l	c	u	l	a	t	e
e	o	h	a	j	x	m	e	n
e	x	p	l	o	r	e	m	s
z	s	i	a	k	r	w	p	e
b	e	l	i	e	v	e	l	s
e	v	u	p	r	o	v	e	t

1 show that something is correct __prove__

2 a special day _____

3 think that something is true _____

4 a building with statues of gods _____

5 look around a new place _____

6 use numbers to find out something _____

7 it can move things _____

3 Complete the sentences.

> discovered   believed   Sun   universe
> gravity   believed   important   proved

1 Copernicus said that everything in the solar system orbited

the _____, but nobody _____ him.

2 Galileo _____ Copernicus, but _____ people
didn't want him to write about his ideas.

3 Newton discovered the force of _____. He _____
that Copernicus was right.

4 Hubble _____ another galaxy. Now we know that

there are lots of galaxies in the _____.

4 Write _true_ or _false_.

1 Ancient people used the stars to calculate things.   _____

2 Galileo thought that the Earth orbited the Sun.   _____

3 Gravity makes planets orbit the Sun.   _____

4 The Milky Way is made of billions of comets.   _____

5 Hubble discovered another universe.   _____

**5 What do you think was the most important discovery in
the history of astronomy? Why?**

_____

_____

_____

_____

_____

6 Life on Other Planets

Read pages 24–27.

1 Write the words.   UFO   canal   bacteria   alien

1 _____

2 _____

3 _____

4 _____

2 Write *Earth*, *Mars*, *Europa*, or *Titan*.

1 These places have an atmosphere.

   ___Earth___ , _____ , and _____

2 The surface of these places is ice.

   _____ and _____

3 Robots are exploring this place.

   _____

4 These places have lakes on the surface.

   _____ and _____

5 Lots of living things are in this place.

   _____

3 Complete the sentences.

> imagine   covers   underground   simple

1 Bacteria are _____ living things on Earth.

2 We can _____ life on other planets.

3 Maybe there are _____ rivers on Mars.

4 Ice _____ the surface of Europa.

4 Circle the correct words.

1 Life on Earth needs **solid** / **liquid** water.

2 At the moment, robots are exploring **Venus** / **Mars**.

3 Scientists think that the inside of Europa is **warmer** / **colder** than the surface.

4 The lakes on Titan are made of **oxygen** / **hydrocarbons**.

5 Answer the questions.

1 Why did people think there were canals on Mars?

_____

2 Why isn't there any water on the surface of Mars?

_____

3 What are living things made of?

_____

4 Do you think we will find life on other planets? Why or why not? _____

_____

7 People in Space

 Read pages 28–31.

orbited   Space Station
~~rocket~~   Moon   person
space shuttle

1 Complete the chart.

The History of Space Travel	
1957	The first ___rocket___ went into space.
1961	The first _____ visited space.
1968	Astronauts in *Apollo 8* _____ the Moon for the first time.
1969	Astronauts landed on the _____ for the first time.
1981	The _____ flew for the first time.
1998	The first astronauts visited the International _____ .

2 Write *true* or *false*.

1 The first person in space was American.   _____

2 Astronauts collected things from the Moon.   _____

3 A space shuttle takes off like a plane.   _____

4 A space station is where astronauts can live.   _____

5 Gravity makes your body strong.   _____

6 The International Space Station was built on Earth.   _____

3 Complete the puzzle.

1 In space, things __ when you don't hold them.
2 Astronauts sleep in a special __ .
3 Astronauts don't feel __ in space.
4 Astronauts have to use __ machines to keep their bodies strong.
5 Astronauts wear a __ to cover their eyes.
6 Astronauts use a special __ because water floats in space.
7 Astronauts cook food in special __ .
8 Astronauts can become __ in space.

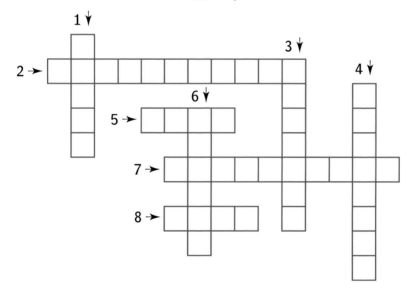

4 Would you like to live in space? Why or why not?

_____

_____

_____

_____

_____

_____

8 Our Future in Space

← Read pages 32–35.

1 Complete the sentences.

Engineers   Radiation   experiments   space suit

1 You have to wear a _____ to protect your body in space.

2 _____ is dangerous energy from the Sun.

3 Scientists will do _____ in the Moon base.

4 _____ are designing new robots.

2 Match. Then write the sentences.

Space planes are	invent faster spacecraft.
Robonauts	stay in space hotels.
Earth's atmosphere	go to dangerous places.
Maybe tourists will	cheaper than rockets.
Scientists will probably	protects us from radiation.

1 _Space planes are cheaper than rockets._

2 _____

3 _____

4 _____

5 _____

3 **Complete the chart.**

exploring other solar systems   robots on Mars   space tourism
finding aliens   space hotels   very fast new spacecraft
a Moon base   space planes   astronauts on Mars

This has happened:
_____
_____
This will happen:
_____
_____
Maybe this will happen one day:
_____
_____

4 **Answer the questions.**

1 What have people built to take tourists into space?

_____

2 When will astronauts go back to the Moon?

_____

3 Why is it easier to use robonauts in dangerous places?

_____

4 What do you think will happen in space in the future?

_____

_____

A Planet Poster

1　Imagine you can visit any planet in the solar system.

2　Choose a planet and write notes.

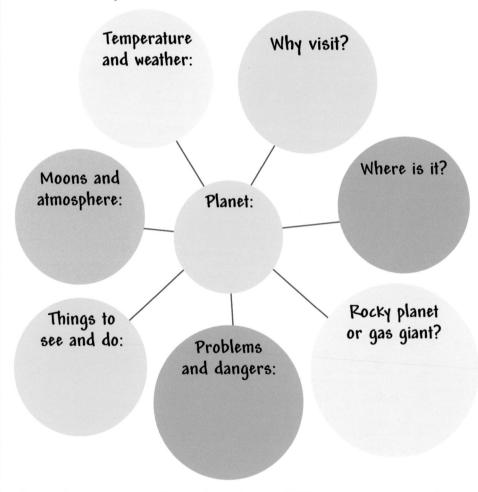

Temperature and weather:

Why visit?

Moons and atmosphere:

Planet:

Where is it?

Things to see and do:

Problems and dangers:

Rocky planet or gas giant?

3　Make a poster about the planet. Write sentences and add pictures to decorate your poster.

4　Display your poster.

A Space Hotel Advert

1 Imagine a new space hotel. Write notes.

1 Is your hotel orbiting Earth or is it on the Moon?

_____

2 How many tourists can stay there?

_____

3 Do they travel there by rocket or space plane?

_____

4 How long do they stay?

_____

5 How is it different from a hotel on Earth?

_____

6 What interesting things can people do in the hotel?

_____

7 Why is your hotel a great place to stay?

_____

2 Make an advert. Write about your hotel and add pictures to decorate your advert.

3 Display your advert.

Glossary

Here are some words used in this book, and you can check what they mean. Use a dictionary to check other new words.

acid a dangerous liquid that can destroy metal and burn skin

alien a living thing from another planet; from another planet

ancient from thousands of years in the past

appear to start to be seen

area part of a place

asteroid a big rock that orbits the Sun

astronomer a person who studies the planets and stars

astronomy studying the planets and stars

atmosphere the gas and clouds around a planet

bacteria very simple living things

believe to think that something is true

belt something that goes around something

bright full of light

burn to make flames and heat

calculate to use numbers to find out something

calendar a record of the months and days in a year

canal it's man-made and like a river

canyon a deep valley

carbon a chemical that is in all living things

center the middle

change to become different; to make something different

chemical a solid or liquid that is made by chemistry

comet a big piece of ice and dust that orbits the Sun

container we put things like food in this

cover to put something over something; to be over something

crater a big hole in the ground made by an explosion

deep going a long way down

destroy to damage something very badly

die to stop living

distance the space between two places

dust very small pieces of dirt

dwarf a very small person or thing

energy we need energy to move and grow; machines need energy to work

enough how much we want or need

enter to go into

equipment things you need, like machines and tools

exercise what we do when we move to stay healthy

exist to live

experiment a test using science equipment

explode to suddenly divide into lots of pieces

explore to travel to new places to discover new things

explosion what you get when something explodes

farthest at the biggest distance

finish to end

float to move slowly on water or in the air

forest a place with a lot of trees

form to make or to be made

fuel something that we use to produce heat or energy

galaxy a very big group of stars in space

gas not a solid or liquid; air is a gas

giant a very big person or thing

gravity this makes small things move toward bigger things in space and pulls things toward the ground on Earth

group a number of people or things that are together

grow to get bigger

hole a space in something

huge very big

hydrocarbon a chemical made of hydrogen, carbon, and other things

imagine to think of a possible situation

inner on the inside

kill to make something or someone die

lake a big area of water

land to fly a plane or rocket from the air onto the land

last to happen for an amount of time

life all things that live, like animals, plants, and people

liquid not a solid; water is a liquid

mask you wear this over your face or your eyes

material something that you use to make other things

metal a hard material made from minerals; rockets and planes are made of this

meteor a material from space that enters a planet's atmosphere

meteorite a material from space that hits a planet

Moon base a place on the Moon for astronauts to live and work

object a thing

orbit to go around something

outer on the outside

oven you cook food inside it

past many years ago

planet a large, round thing in space that goes around a star

plant to put seeds or plants in the soil to make them grow

pressure the force or weight of something on another thing

process when things happen one after another

produce to make something

protect to keep safe from danger

prove to show that something is true

reach to get to

real that exists

ring a circle

rise to go up

rocky with a lot of rocks

satellite a machine that goes into space

seed the small, hard part of a plant; a new plant can grow from this

set to go down

shower you wash yourself with this

single one

size how big or small something or someone is

sky where the clouds and the Sun are

soil the ground that plants grow in

solar system a sun with planets around it

space everything around Earth and outside Earth's atmosphere

spacecraft a machine that travels through space

space shuttle a spacecraft that can go into space many times

space station a place in space for astronauts to live in

space suit special clothes that protect astronauts

spot a round shape

statue a man-made shape of a person, often made of stone

step to put your feet on something

stick to join one thing to another

storm bad weather; lots of wind and rain

sunrise when the Sun comes up in the morning

surface the outside or the top of something

tail a long thing behind an animal or a comet

take off to leave the ground

technology the design of new machines

telescope a machine that makes things look bigger

temperature how hot or cold something is

temple a religious building

trap to keep something in a place where it can't escape

UFO an unidentified flying object; we don't know what this is

universe everything that exists in space and time

view the things that you can see from a place like a window

weight how heavy something is

Oxford Read and Discover

Series Editor: Hazel Geatches • CLIL Adviser: John Clegg

Oxford Read and Discover graded readers are at six levels, for students from age 6 and older. They cover many topics within three subject areas, and support English across the curriculum, or Content and Language Integrated Learning (CLIL).

Available for each reader:
• Audio Pack
• Activity Book

Available for selected readers:
• e-Books

Teaching notes & CLIL guidance: **www.oup.com/elt/teacher/readanddiscover**

Subject Area / Level	The World of Science & Technology	The Natural World	The World of Arts & Social Studies
1 300 headwords	• Eyes • Fruit • Trees • Wheels	• At the Beach • In the Sky • Wild Cats • Young Animals	• Art • Schools
2 450 headwords	• Electricity • Plastic • Sunny and Rainy • Your Body	• Camouflage • Earth • Farms • In the Mountains	• Cities • Jobs
3 600 headwords	• How We Make Products • Sound and Music • Super Structures • Your Five Senses	• Amazing Minibeasts • Animals in the Air • Life in Rainforests • Wonderful Water	• Festivals Around the World • Free Time Around the World
4 750 headwords	• All About Plants • How to Stay Healthy • Machines Then and Now • Why We Recycle	• All About Desert Life • All About Ocean Life • Animals at Night • Incredible Earth	• Animals in Art • Wonders of the Past
5 900 headwords	• Materials to Products • Medicine Then and Now • Transportation Then and Now • Wild Weather	• All About Islands • Animal Life Cycles • Exploring Our World • Great Migrations	• Homes Around the World • Our World in Art
6 1,050 headwords	• Cells and Microbes • Clothes Then and Now • Incredible Energy • Your Amazing Body	• All About Space • Caring for Our Planet • Earth Then and Now • Wonderful Ecosystems	• Food Around the World • Helping Around the World

	Metric measurement	Customary measurement
Page 5	150 million kilometers	93 million miles
Page 7	2,500 kilometers	1,553 miles
Page 8	427 degrees centigrade	800 degrees Fahrenheit
	-173 degrees centigrade	-279 degrees Fahrenheit
Page 9	462 degrees centigrade	864 degrees Fahrenheit
Page 11	25 kilometers	15.5 miles
Page 15	2.4 billion kilometers	1.5 billion miles
	2 billion kilometers	1.2 billion miles
	-214 degrees centigrade	-353 degrees Fahrenheit
Page 17	50 kilometers	31 miles
Page 18	1,000 metric tons	1,100 tons
Page 19	20 kilometers	12.4 miles
	180 kilometers	112 miles
Page 33	386,000 kilometers	239,849 miles

Oxford Read and Discover

All About Space

Alex Raynham

Read and discover all about our galaxy and everything in the universe …

- What are the stars made of?
- When did the first person walk on the Moon?

Word count for this reader: 3,820 words

Read and discover more about the world! This series of non-fiction readers provides interesting and educational content, with activities and project work.

Series Editor: Hazel Geatches

Also available:
- ◀)) Audio Pack
- 🖹 Activity Book
- 🗎 e-Book

You can also enjoy this fiction book from **Oxford Read and Imagine.**

The Secret on the Moon

Cover image: Alamy (Astronaut taking a spacewalk/NASA)

OXFORD
UNIVERSITY PRESS

www.oup.com/elt

CEFR
B1
A2
A1

ISBN 978-0-19-464560-7

9 780194 645607